Animal Tracks

OF THE SOUTHWEST

Covers more than 150 species!

Adventure Quick Guides

by Jonathan Poppele

Adventure Quick Guides

Organized by track group for quick and easy identification, this guide has 59 entries covering more than 150 species of four-legged mammals commonly found in the Southwest.

HELPFUL NOTES FOR USING THIS QUICK GUIDE:

- Use the Tracking Tips to learn about the basics of tracking and the Track Group Chart to determine which group a track belongs to. These supplements are at the back of the book.

- Individual tracks show a great deal of variation. Use track size and gait (track pattern) as additional clues when identifying a print.

- The measurements in this guide represent an average range for the species. Individual prints may vary from these ranges, especially in soft or loose ground such as snow, sand or mud.

- The most common gait is shown for each species. Some species, such as tree squirrels, show little variation. Other species, such as coyotes, display a wide variety of gaits.

SOUTHWEST PLAYING CARDS

For more information about animal tracks, look for Jonathan Poppele's *Animal Tracks of the Southwest* playing cards!

ABOUT THE AUTHOR

Jonathan Poppele is an award-winning nature guidebook author and naturalist, and he has been studying tracking throughout the United States since 1995. You can contact him at www.mntracking.org

10 9 8 7 6 5 4 3

Cover design by Jonathan Norberg, interior design by Lora Westberg.

All images copyrighted.
Images by contributing photographers: Rick and Nora Bowers, Mary Clay/Dembinsky Photo Associates, Jerry Dragoo, John Kormendy/University of Texas at Austin, Maslowski Wildlife Productions, Ann and Rob Simpson and Stan Tekiela.

The following (altered) image is licensed according to the Creative Commons 2.0 Attribution License, which is available here: https://creativecommons.org/licenses/by/2.0/. Page 5: "Hispid cotton rat" by Flickr User Stephen Pollard. Original image available here: www.flickr.com/photos/stephen_pollard/4274961667/

Illustrations by Julie Martinez and Bruce Wilson.

Animal Tracks of the Southwest
Copyright © 2016 by Jonathan Poppele
All rights reserved
Printed in China

Harvest Mice

FRONT: L ¼"–⅜"; W ¼"–⁵⁄₁₆"
HIND: L ¼"–½"; W ³⁄₁₆"–⁵⁄₁₆"

The "thumb" on the hind foot is set
farther back than in other mice.

White-footed Mice

FRONT: L ¼"–½"; W ⁵⁄₁₆"–½"
HIND: L ¼"–⁹⁄₁₆"; W ⁵⁄₁₆"–½"

Very common. Leave a trail pattern
like that of a miniature squirrel.

House Mouse

FRONT: L ¼"–½"; W ⁵⁄₁₆"–½"
HIND: L ¼"–⁹⁄₁₆"; W ⁵⁄₁₆"–½"

Common in and around
buildings. Usually walks
rather than bounds.

Voles & Lemmings

FRONT: L ¼"–½"; W ¼"–½"
HIND: L ¼"–⅝"; W ¼"–½"

Found around fresh vegetation.
Usually walk rather than bound.

Tiny Mammals

Shrews
FRONT: L ³⁄₁₆"–⁵⁄₁₆"; W ³⁄₁₆"–⁵⁄₁₆"
HIND: L ³⁄₁₆"–⁷⁄₁₆"; W ³⁄₁₆"–⁵⁄₁₆"

Tiny, delicate tracks are only visible under ideal conditions.

Moles
FRONT: L ³⁄₈"–⁵⁄₈"; W ³⁄₈"–⁵⁄₈"
HIND: L ¼"–½"; W ¼"–½"

Tracks are rarely seen. Digging signs are quite obvious.

Jumping Mice
FRONT: L ³⁄₈"–⁵⁄₈"; W ³⁄₈"–⁵⁄₈"
HIND: L ½"–1⅛"; W ³⁄₈"–¾"

Hibernate through the winter in colder climates. Have extremely long, slender toes.

Pocket Mice
FRONT: L ¼"–³⁄₈"; W ¼"–³⁄₈"
HIND: L ³⁄₈"–½"; W ¼"–½"

Only four toes show clearly on the hind foot. Pads are often indistinct.

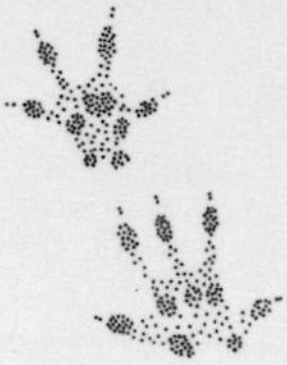

Cotton Rats

FRONT: L 3/8"–1/2"; W 3/8"–1/2"
HIND: L 7/16"–11/16"; W 7/16"–9/16"

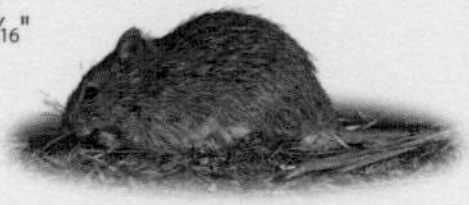

Tracks are larger than mouse tracks but smaller than Old World rat tracks.

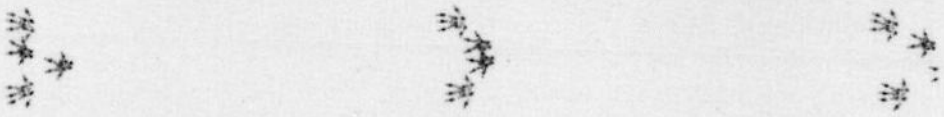

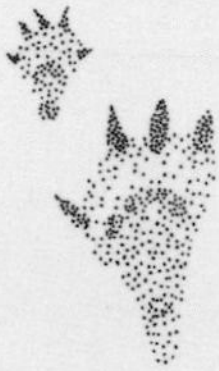

Kangaroo Rats

FRONT: L 1/4"–1/2"; W 1/4"–3/8"
HIND: L 3/8"–1 1/4"; W 3/8"–3/4"

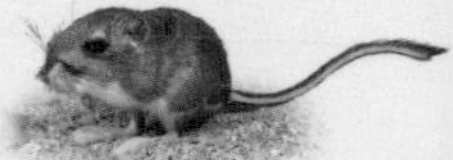

Usually leave only hind prints. Hind tracks show only four toes.

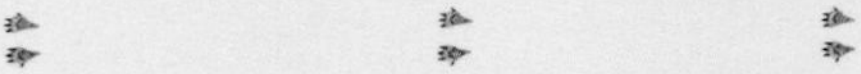

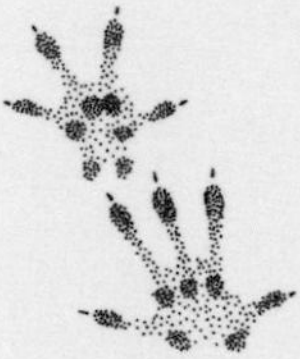

Old World Rats

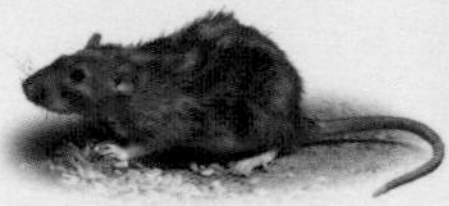

FRONT: L 1/2"–3/4"; W 1/2"–3/4"
HIND: L 5/8"–1 1/4"; W 5/8"–1"

Common around buildings. Tracks are mouse-like but much larger.

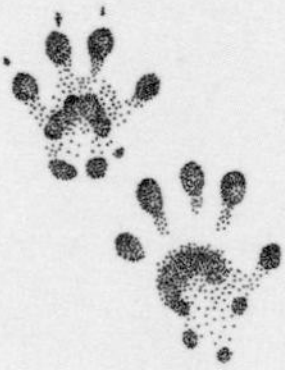

Woodrats

FRONT: L 3/8"–7/8"; W 3/8"–3/4"
HIND: L 1/2"–1 1/4"; W 1/2"–7/8"

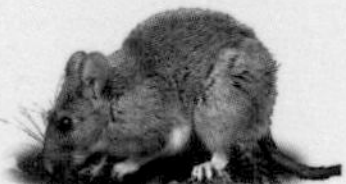

More bulbous toe pads than other small rodents.

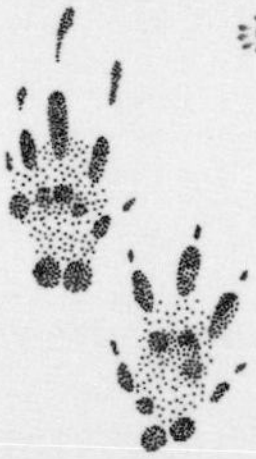

Pocket Gophers

FRONT: L 3/4"–1 1/4"; W 3/8"–7/8"
HIND: L 7/8"–1 1/8"; W 3/8"–7/8"

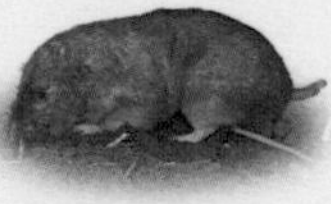

Digging signs are often conspicuous, but tracks are uncommon.

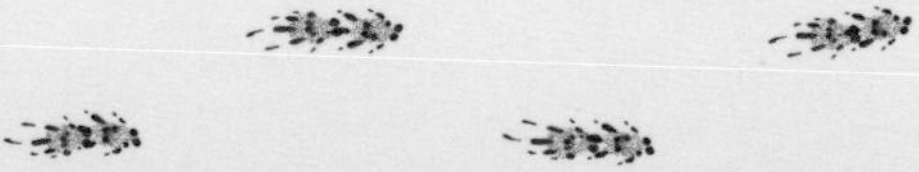

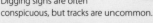

Chipmunks

FRONT: L ½"–⅞"; W ⅜"–¾"
HIND: L ⅜"–1"; W ⅜"–⅞"

Tracks and trails are similar to those of tree squirrels, but smaller.

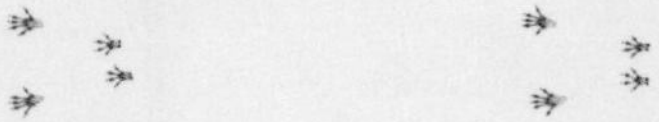

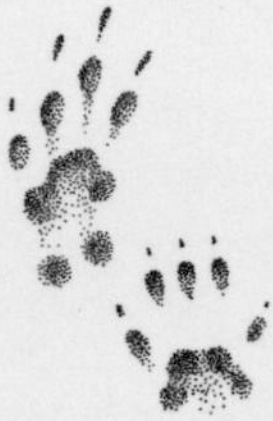

Ground Squirrels

FRONT: L ½"–1⅜"; W ⅜"–1"
HIND: L ⅝"–1½"; W ½"–1⅜"

Front tracks have prominent claws. Many species are inactive during the hottest and coldest times of the year.

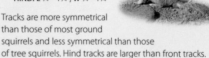

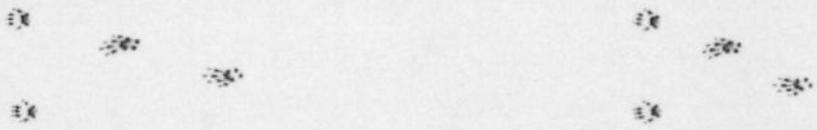

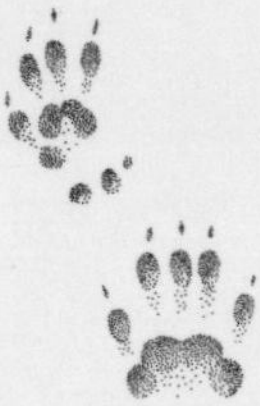

Rock Squirrel

FRONT: L ¾"–1¼"; W ⅝"–1"
HIND: L ¾"–1¼"; W ¾"–1¼"

Tracks are more symmetrical than those of most ground squirrels and less symmetrical than those of tree squirrels. Hind tracks are larger than front tracks.

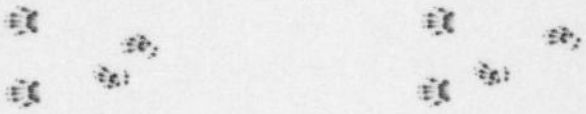

Prairie Dogs

FRONT: L 1"–1½"; W ⅞"–1⅜"
HIND: L 1"–2"; W ⅞"–1⅜"

Live in large, unmistakable communal burrows.

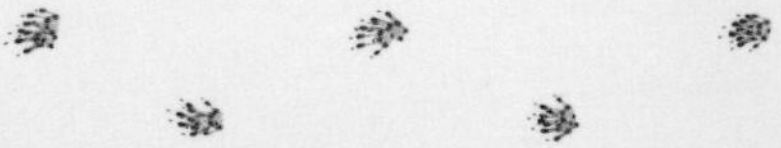

Southern Flying Squirrel

FRONT: L ⅜"–¾"; W ⅜"–¾"
HIND: L ½"–1⅜"; W ⅜"–⅞"

Feet are heavily furred. Usually hops rather than bounds.

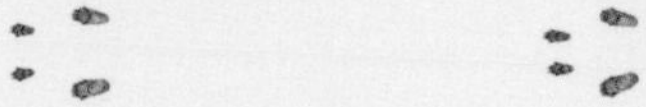

Northern Flying Squirrel

FRONT: L ½"–1"; W ½"–¾"
HIND: L 1¼"–1¾"; W ⅝"–⅞"

Front feet usually land wide apart, creating a "boxy" track pattern.

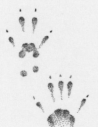

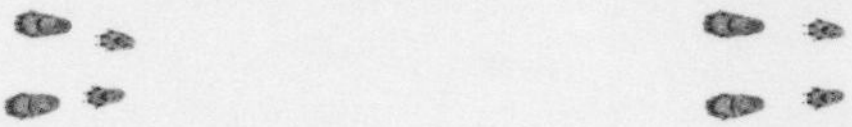

Pine Squirrels

FRONT: L ⅞"–1¼"; W ½"–1"
HIND: L 1"–2"; W ¾"–1¼"

Distinctive squirrel tracks and trails. Their tracks are larger than a chipmunk's and smaller than a tree squirrel's.

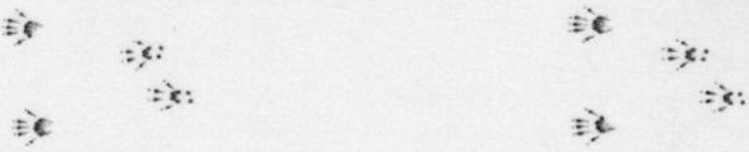

Tree Squirrels

FRONT: L 1"–1¾"; W ½"–1½"
HIND: L 1"–2¾"; W ⅞"–1¾"

Distinctive squirrel trail patterns. Trails usually begin and end at trees.

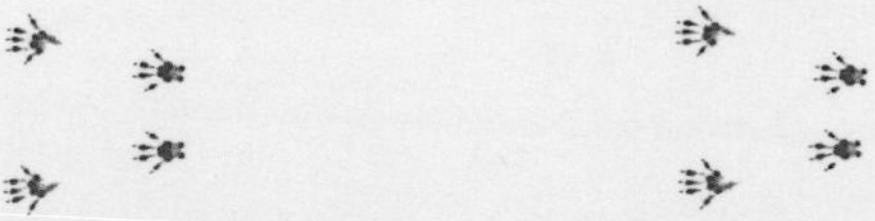

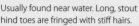

Large Rodents

Muskrat
FRONT: L 1"–1½"; W 1"–1½"
HIND: L 1½"–2½"; W 1⅜"–2¼"

Usually found near water. Long, stout hind toes are fringed with stiff hairs.

Yellow-bellied Marmot
FRONT: L 1½"–2¾"; W 1¼"–2"
HIND: L 1⅜"–3"; W 1¼"–2"

Large, squirrel-like tracks. Typically walks rather than bounds.

North American Porcupine
FRONT: L 2¼"–3¼"; W 1½"–1⅞"
HIND: L 2¾"–4"; W 1¼"–2"

Oval tracks with a unique "pebbly" texture. Toes rarely show.

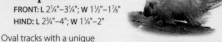

American Beaver
FRONT: L 2"–3½"; W 1½"–3"
HIND: L 4½"–7"; W 3"–5"

Clear hind prints are unmistakable. Trails usually lead to or from water.

Pika, Rabbits & Hares

American Pika
FRONT: L ⅝"–¾"; W ⅝"–¾"
HIND: L ⅝"–1"; W ⅝"–⅞"

Lives in rocky terrain at high elevations. Clear prints are rare.

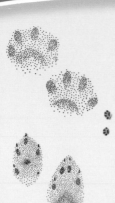

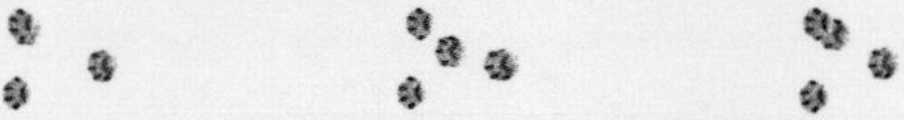

Cottontail Rabbits
FRONT: L ⅞"–1¾"; W ⅝"–1¼"
HIND: L 1¼"–3¼"; W ¾"–1⅝"

Very common. Egg-shaped tracks. Distinctive rabbit trail pattern.

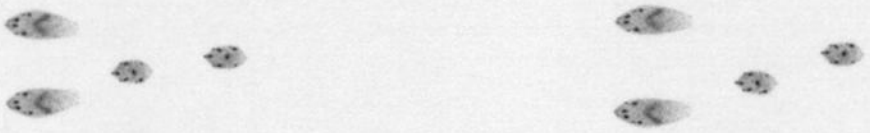

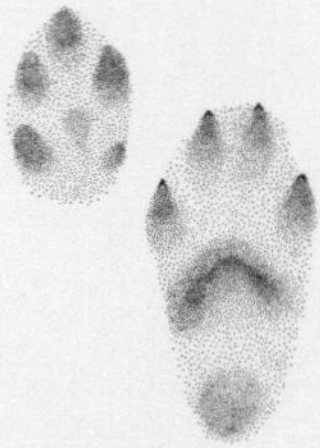

Snowshoe Hare
FRONT: L 1¾"–3"; W 1¼"–2¼"
HIND: L 3"–5"; W 1½"–4½"

Hind tracks can be much larger than front. Distinctive rabbit trail pattern.

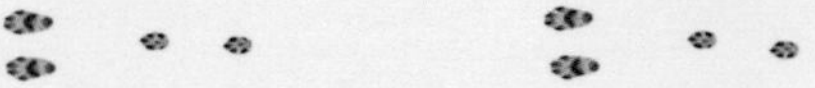

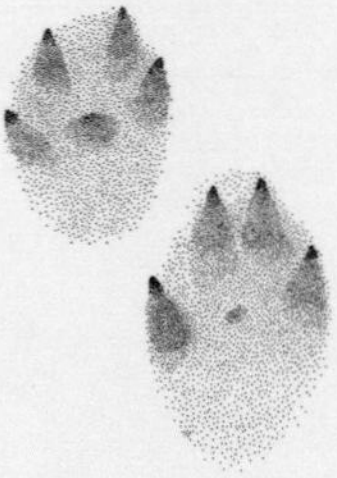

Black-tailed Jackrabbit
FRONT: L 1⅝"–2½"; W 1¼"–1¾"
HIND: L 2"–5"; W 1¼"–2½"

Hind heel rarely shows. Has a broader range of gaits than most other rabbits.

White-tailed Jackrabbit
FRONT: L 2⅛"–3¾"; W 1½"–2½"
HIND: L 3"–6½"; W 1½"–3"

Hind heel rarely shows. Hind tracks are typically offset from each other.

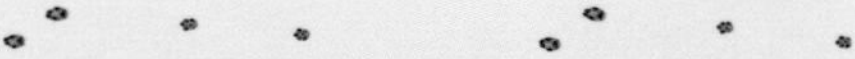

Nine-banded Armadillo

FRONT: L 1½"–2"; W 1"–1¾"
HIND: L 2"–3"; W 1½"–2¼"

Tracks have a distinctive birdlike appearance.

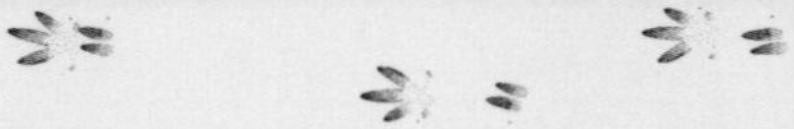

Skunks

Spotted Skunks

FRONT: L 1"–1⅜"; W ¾"–1"
HIND: L ¾"–1¼"; W ⅝"–1⅛"

Tracks have clean, compact look. Prominent claws. Irregular gaits.

Striped & Hooded Skunks

FRONT: L ⅞"–1¾"; W ⅞"–1¼"
HIND: L 1"–1¾"; W ⅞"–1¼"

Prominent claws. Toes never splay. Trails resemble those of a miniature bear.

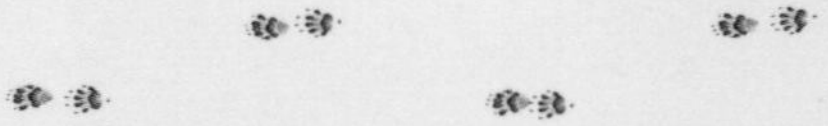

Hog-nosed Skunk

FRONT: L ¾"–1¾"; W 1¼"–1½"
HIND: L 1"–1½"; W 1⅛"–1¾"

Prominent claws. Tracks are larger and more symmetrical than in other skunks. May look like badger tracks.

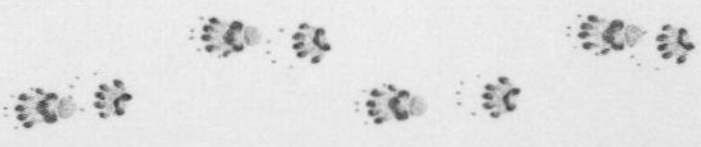

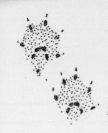

Weasels

FRONT: L ⁵⁄₁₆"–½"; W ⁵⁄₁₆"–½"
HIND: L ⁵⁄₁₆"–½"; W ⁵⁄₁₆"–½"

Small tracks, typically in a 2x2 lope with highly variable strides.

American Mink

FRONT: L 1"–1¾"; W ¾"–1⅝"
HIND: L ¾"–1½"; W ⅞"–1⅝"

Crisper tracks than other small weasels. Usually found close to water.

American Badger

FRONT: L 1⅞"–2⅝"; W 1½"–2¾"
HIND: L 1½"–2½"; W 1¼"–2¼"

Walks with toes turned in. Long claws leave prominent marks.

Northern River Otter

FRONT: L 2"–3"; W 1⅞"–3"
HIND: L 2¼"–3¾"; W 2⅛"–3½"

Usually found near water. Trails often include slides. May show tail drag.

Five-toed Walkers

Virginia Opossum
FRONT: L 1¼"–2⅛"; W 1½"–2¼" 
HIND: L 1½"–2½"; W 1½"–2⅝"

Front track has starlike shape.
Hind track resembles a human hand.

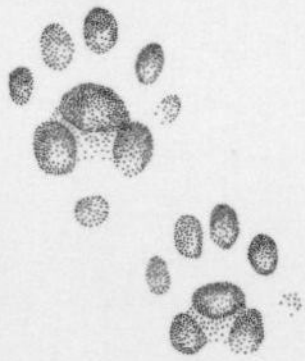

Ringtail
FRONT: L 1"–1½"; W 1"–1⅜"
HIND: L 1"–1½"; W ⅞"–1¼"

Tracks resemble those of
house cats but have a larger
palm pad. Claws rarely register.

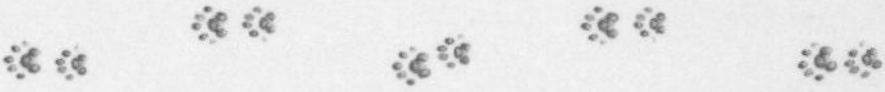

White-nosed Coati
FRONT: L 1½"–2⅝"; W 1¼"–1⅞"
HIND: L 2¼"–3¼"; W 1⅜"–2"

Similar to raccoon tracks. Front
tracks have longer, stouter claws
and show heel pads more often.

Northern Raccoon
FRONT: L 1¾"–2¾"; W 1½"–2¾" 
HIND: L 2"–2¾"; W 1½"–2¾"

Distinctive 2x2 walking gait. Tracks
often resemble human handprints.

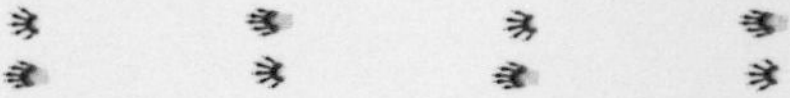

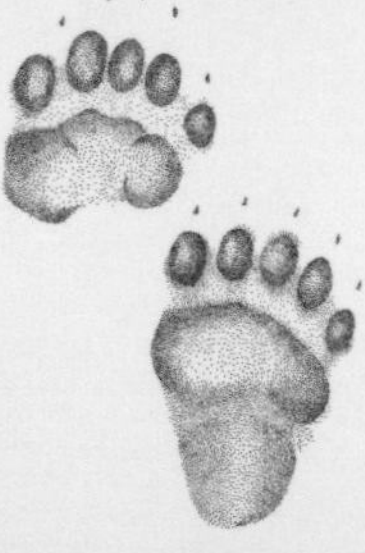

Black Bear
FRONT: L 3½"–6"; W 3½"–5½" 
HIND: L 5"–8"; W 3½"–5¾"

Five toes and robust palm
pads. Very large. Clear prints
are unmistakable.

Swift Fox & Kit Fox

FRONT: L 1"–1½"; W 1"–1½"
HIND: L 1"–1½"; W ⅞"–1¼"

Smallest wild canine tracks in the Southwest. Hind palm may not register.

Gray Fox

FRONT: L 1¼"–1¾"; W 1¼"–1¾"
HIND: L 1⅛"–1¾"; W 1"–1⅝"

Claws may not show. Trails may begin or end at the base of a tree.

Red Fox

FRONT: L 1¾"–2½"; W 1½"–2⅛"
HIND: L 1½"–2½"; W 1¼"–1⅞"

Heavy fur often makes pads less distinct than those of other canines.

Coyote

FRONT: L 2"–3"; W 1½"–2¾"
HIND: L 2"–3"; W 1⅜"–2¼"

Tracks usually narrower than in other canines. Hind palm may not register.

House Cat
FRONT: L 1"–1⅝"; W 1"–1¾"
HIND: L 1⅛"–1⅝"; W ⅞"–1⅝"

Tracks are round with a large palm pad. Claws rarely show.

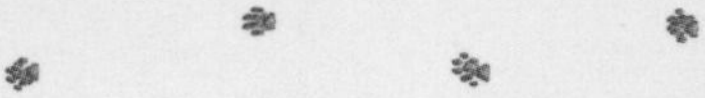

Bobcat
FRONT: L 1½"–2½"; W 1½"–2½"
HIND: L 1½"–2½"; W 1¼"–2¼"

Asymmetrical front track may be wider than it is long. Large palm pads.

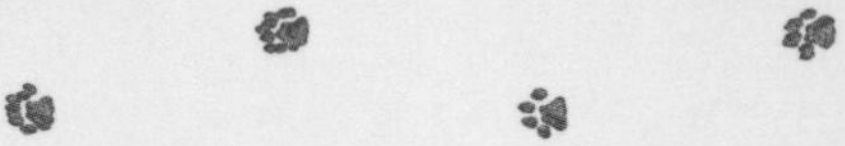

Cougar
FRONT: L 2¾"–4"; W 2¾"–4½"
HIND: L 2¾"–4"; W 2½"–4¼"

Large palm pad. The largest track in our region that doesn't show claws.

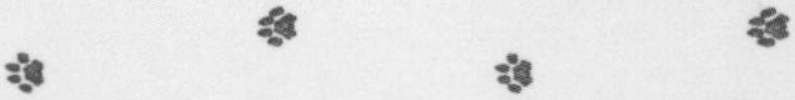

Pronghorn
FRONT: L 2⅛"–3¼"; W 1½"–2⅜"
HIND: L 2⅛"–3"; W 1½"–2⅛"

Narrow, heart-shaped track. Center of the track is often slightly raised.

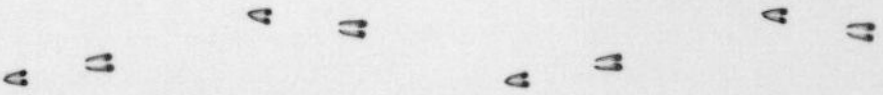

Collared Peccary
FRONT: L ⅞"–2"; W ¾"–2" 
HIND: L ¾"–1¾"; W ¾"–1¾"

Tracks are smaller than a feral pig's. Its dust baths/wallows often have an "old cheese" odor.

Feral Pigs
FRONT: L 2"–2½"; W 2⅛"–2¾"
HIND: L 1¾"–2¼"; W 1¾"–2¼"

Leave prominent signs of rooting for food. Turn up earth and do considerable damage to vegetation.

Deer
FRONT: L 2"–3½"; W 1⅝"–2¾"
HIND: L 1⅞"–3¼"; W 1½"–2½"

Extremely abundant. Distinctive and familiar heart-shaped track.

Elk
FRONT: L 3¼"–4¾"; W 2¾"–4¼"
HIND: L 2⅞"–4¼"; W 2⅜"–3¾"

Large tracks are rounder than those of other members of the deer family.

Bighorn Sheep
FRONT: L 2¼"–3⅜"; W 2"–2¾"
HIND: L 2¼"–3⅜"; W 1¼"–2½"

Always found on or near steep, rocky slopes. Tracks similar to deer tracks, with more rounded toes.

Domestic Cow
FRONT: L 2½"–4¾"; W 2¼"–5¾"
HIND: L 2½"–4¾"; W 2¼"–4¾"

Large, round tracks. Typically smaller than bison but not always distinguishable.

Bison
FRONT: L 4½"–6½"; W 4½"–6½"
HIND: L 4"–6"; W 4"–6"

Enormous round hoof prints can only be mistaken for tracks of domestic cattle.

Horse
FRONT: L 4¾"–5½"; W 4¼"–5¼"
HIND: L 4½"–5¼"; W 4"–4¾"

Large, round, single-toed tracks are unmistakable.

Individual Track Identification

When looking at individual prints, identify both the front and hind tracks of the animal, if possible. Once you do, these four steps can help you identify the track:

1. Study the overall shape of the track
2. Count the number of toes
3. Look for claws
4. Measure the size of the track

STEP 1. STUDY THE OVERALL SHAPE OF THE TRACK

Is the track circular, oval or lopsided? Is it wider at the front or wider at the back? Are the toes symmetrically or asymmetrically arranged?

STEP 2. COUNT THE NUMBER OF TOES

Be careful—there are a lot of things that can confound this seemingly simple task. One or more toes may not register clearly, or toes may be set far off to the side. Stray marks on the ground may look like toes. Try to find a couple of prints from the same foot to verify your count.

STEP 3. LOOK FOR CLAWS

Some animals, like dogs and skunks, nearly always show claw marks. Others rarely do. While not foolproof, presence or absence of claws is a useful clue for identification.

STEP 4. MEASURE THE SIZE OF THE TRACK

Measure the track's length and width. While animal foot sizes can vary tremendously within a species, track size will help you narrow down the possibilities.

HOW TO MEASURE TRACKS

Measure tracks along their longest and widest points. Measure length from the rear edge of the rearmost palm or heel pad to the front edge of the foremost toe pad. The measurements in this guide do not include claws unless they are indistinguishable from the toes or unless the toes themselves are not visible. Measure width across the widest part of the foot, including all of the toes. Note: Getting accurate measurements can be tricky. Momentum can distort the length of the track; soft ground, sand and snow can alter track size; and uneven ground can skew shape. Look for clear tracks relatively free from distortion. If you can, measure several tracks to get an average.

Gaits

Gaits describe the body mechanics of an animal's movement, including the order of its footfalls and how it coordinates its limbs. Each gait leaves a distinctive pattern of tracks. Most mammals in the Southwest walk on all fours. Four-legged movement is more complicated than two-legged movement and requires some special terminology. Four-legged gaits can be broadly divided into two categories: whole-body gaits and stepping gaits.

WHOLE-BODY GAITS

In whole-body gaits, the body flexes and extends, and movement is created by the torso and legs working together. These gaits have a syncopated rhythm and produce distinctive groups of four tracks. Whole-body gaits fall into two categories: those where each foot lands independently, called lopes and gallops, and those where the hind feet land together, called hops and bounds.

Loping and Galloping: In both lopes and gallops, each foot moves independently as the animal flexes and extends its body. In a lope, at least one hind foot lands behind one of the front feet. In gallops, both hind feet land in front of the front feet. Lopes can be easy, gentle gaits, while gallops are usually all-out sprints. Lopes are the most common gaits for members of the weasel family.

Skunk lope

Red Fox gallop

Hopping and Bounding: Hops and bounds are distinguished in the same way as lopes and gallops. A gait is a hop when the hind tracks are behind one front track and a bound when they are in front of the front tracks. When bounding, an animal's hind feet straddle its front feet, causing the hind tracks to register wider than in the front. Tree-climbing animals usually bound with their front feet side-by-side, while non-climbers usually place one front foot ahead of the other. Bounding is the most common gait for most small rodents and most members of the rabbit family.

Squirrel bound

Cottontail bound

STEPPING GAITS

In stepping gaits, an animal keeps its body level and uses only its legs for locomotion. The legs move with an even rhythm and produce a line of evenly spaced pairs of tracks. Stepping gaits can be divided into walks and trots.

Walking: When walking, an animal moves each leg independently and always has at least one foot on the ground. Animals can place their hind feet on the ground either behind their front track (understep), on top of it (direct register) or in front of it (overstep). Raccoons use an extreme overstep, placing their hind foot next to the front track on the opposite side of the body. Walking is the most common gait for bears, raccoons, some large rodents and members of the cat and deer family.

Deer walk

Raccoon walk

Trotting: When an animal trots, the two legs diagonally opposite each other move at the same time, and there is a split second when then animal has all four feet off the ground. Like walks, trots can be understep, direct register or overstep. Overstep trots generally require the animal to turn its body slightly, allowing the hind feet to pass to the side of the front feet. Trots are the most common gaits for members of the dog family, as well as some voles and shrews.

Coyote trot

Fox side-trot

Photographing Tracks

- **Shoot in the Shade:** Dappled sun is difficult to expose properly; shadows can distort the shape of the track.

- **Get Close:** Your track or track group should fill your frame. Use a macro setting if possible.

- **Include a Scale:** This helps you judge track size.

- **Shoot Straight Down:** Shooting at even a slight angle can distort a track's shape and apparent size.

- **Shoot at Different Exposures:** Many built-in light meters are fooled by sand, snow and mud. Experiment with adjusting the exposure.

- **Take Lots of Pictures:** Take lots of pictures using different settings, then pick out the best to keep.

- **Take Pictures of the Trail and the Surroundings:** Your photographic record will be more useful if you include pictures of the animal's trail and the landscape that it was passing through.

- **Take Notes:** Record where and when you took a picture, as well as information about the surrounding area, for context.

Track Group Chart

Track Group	STEP 1: Overall Shape	STEP 2: Number of Toes	STEP 3: Claws Show?	
TINY MAMMALS	Tracks generally well under 1"	4 or 5 (front) 5 (hind)	Yes	
SQUIRRELS	Triangular palm pad, long toes; front foot often shows 2 heel pads	4 (front) 5 (hind)	Yes	
LARGE RODENTS	Each track in this group is distinctive	4 (front) 5 (hind)	Yes	
PIKA, RABBITS & HARES	Egg-shaped; pads usually indistinct	4 (front) 4 (hind)	Yes, may be obscure	
ARMADILLO	Unique birdlike tracks; outer toes rarely register	4 (front) 5 (hind)	No	
SKUNKS	Compact; stubby toes rarely splay	5 (front) 5 (hind)	Yes	
WEASELS	Toes form an arc above chevron-shaped palm pad	5 (front) 5 (hind)	Yes	
FIVE-TOED WALKERS	Often resemble human hand- or footprints	5 (front) 5 (hind)	Yes	
DOGS	Oval, large, triangular palm pad; claws usually show	4 (front) 4 (hind)	Yes	
CATS	Round, very large, triangular palm pad; retractable claws rarely show	4 (front) 4 (hind)	No	
UNGULATES	Round or heart-shaped hoof prints	1 or 2 (front) 1 or 2 (hind)	Dewclaws	

Adventure Quick Guides

Only Southwest Mammal Tracks

Organized by group for quick
and easy identification

**Simple and convenient—narrow your choices
by group, and view just a few tracks at a time**

- Pocket-sized format—easier than laminated foldouts
- Realistic track illustrations with size information
- More than 150 species found in the Southwest
- Step-by-step guide to track identification
- Track information chart and sample gait patterns

Improve your tracking skills with
Animal Tracks playing cards

ISBN 978-1-59193-587-2 **U.S. $9.95**

5 0 9 9 5

PUBLICATIONS

an imprint of AdventureKEEN

**NATURE / ANIMALS /
SOUTHWEST**

9 781591 935872